Power Within

The Woman

Ms Wattuck -
Oh, how I enjoy
85 South Out + About!
I would _love_ the opportunity
to write for this fine
publication!

Dorothi!

Power Within The Woman

By Dorothy Spearman Clark

Atop Accomplishment, Sat a Woman that Fought.
Beneath Hope, Stooped a Woman that Sought.
Behind Success, Stood a Woman Compelled.
Beside Attainment, Nudged a Woman that Led.
In front of Endeavor, Led a Woman Determined.
All the Above Made Possible,
Due to "Power Within" *__That__* WOMAN!

Proverbs 31:10 Who can find a virtuous Woman? for her price [is] far above rubies.

L.C. & S. Publishing
All Rights Reserved

Copyright © 2004 – Dorothy Spearman Clark
Power Within The Woman – Trademark 2004
Cover Design – Up A Notch Photography and Printing
Text Design – Darlene Newkirk, Brentwood Press

Printed By:
Brentwood Christian Press
4000 Beallwood Avenue
Columbus, Georgia 31904

ISBN 1-59581-074-9

Dedication

This book is dedicated mainly to God, who is first and foremost in my life! Then, I dedicate these writings to my Mother, Mary, my Father Edward James and loving Stepmother, Lois, who is now deceased. May you forever rest in peace.

There are no words that can summate what I feel about those who inspired me to write. Not in the sense of sitting me down and making me take a pen and paper in hand; but, those who inspired my life so much and made me so full that I just have to give recognition to them. I thank God for you; for, I know that it was within his plan that all you spiritual players surrounding me in the tenure of my days here on Earth are those who were sent and meant to edify my being. I will always remember you Ms. Bussey at R.L. Craddock Elementary School, which used to stand on Gray Street in northwest Atlanta; and Ms. Stanford, my 8th Grade English teacher, you have left a lasting memory of well-taught lessons in writing, which will be forever etched in my mind.

I dedicate this book to my spiritual leaders. From the very first, Rev. H.D. Freeman of Zion Grove Baptist Church on Pryor rd. in Atlanta, Georgia and First Lady Estella Freeman. I remember from a child, up to my young adult years great words of inspiration through your many sermons. Those sermons are what sparked my hunger for the Word. Thank you!

Dr. Creflo Dollar and Pastor Taffi Dollar of World Changers Ministries in College Park, Georgia, I thank you for instilling in me words, which were indeed delivered with simplicity and understanding. Your teachings have always been and still are truly a blessing in my life!

My dear friend Pastor Clinton Elder at the Fellowship Christian Center in Newnan, Georgia; you are the warm and gentle leader that God sent to befriend my husband. I thank you for your kind and gentle nature which shows that from deep within, you are the true and devoted friend, placed by God, into our lives. Your Church has truly been a blessing and I thank you First Lady Eva, for your kind words of warmth and encouragement. Minister Marvin, Prophetess Latimer and Apostle, thank you for the circle of love I feel each and every time I enter the Church.

To my sister Juanita and sister Tina; my brothers Dwayne, Felix, Darrell and Ivan; Aunt Louise, Aunt Becky, Auntie Martha, Aunt Odessa, Auntie Annie Ruth, Aunt Pearline, Aunt Louise; friends: Diane, Mike, Roz, and Pearline Bolton; my family members: Valerie J, Waynette, Valerie C, Larry, Bo, Sandra, Barbara Ann, Theresa, Pam, Deon, Reggie, Robbie, Shawn, Kevin, Andre, Lynn, Terry, Tina and Cousin Dee Dee. I love you, not only because you are family, but because you give me a gift of love, each time I am in your presence.

To a good and faithful family friend, Russell Morrison, Sr. – you are great! Ricky Stephenson, you have been a wonderful friend, not only to L.C., but to me as well! Charles of Tampa, Florida and Wayne of College Park, thank you for all the help to our family. Randy, you are my friend. I love you Emanuel. Pamela, Valerie, Audrey and Martha of Friendship Christian Center, you are my new-found friends that I will cherish and love, forever.

And last, but indeed not least: L.C., God knew just what he was doing, when he placed you in my life!

My children, from the oldest to the youngest, from the biological to the inherited, they are: Jeremiah, Bernard, Derrick, Darlena, Angel, Clarissa, Faith, Zsanee, John, Jr, James, Walt, Lo, Chris and Russell, Jr.

I love you, grandchildren! God Bless you all!

Foreword

As I sit here at the typewriter, typing away at the words of this *documentary of a Woman's soul*, I know that God will give me the wisdom and the knowledge to illustrate through these words, the *Power that is Within The Woman.*

I consider myself blessed to be one in this gender. I am blessed to fulfill God's will and purpose in the life of the Woman – a purpose which includes being helpmate, mother, sister and friend. So graciously were we brought forth into creation from the rib of man - how significant a form of humanity! We play a major role in the lives of God's people; though sometimes going about life not ever realizing the magnificent blessings that we possess. For some of us, by the time we realize our full potential, we will have already let the many opportunities to display our Father's miraculous feats pass by. By this time, we will have sat hopeless and defeated on many occasions. We will have wept late at night due to despair. We will have sat lonely and confused -- all due to our lack of opening the windows of our souls and releasing this Power that *already* resides within us.

When I first revealed to my family and friends that I had written "Power Within the Woman", it came as a surprise to most. It was obvious that the majority of people I revealed this heart-felt writing to did not consider the blessing that might be relayed through this book written by a *"common"* Woman. There were those who did not believe that I had been <u>taught</u> to *"know how to"* relate my life situations to the scriptures that I've pointed out in this book; there were others who thought that I had no experience. I even received comments from the peanut gallery that since I hadn't been under any spiritual leader's <u>personal</u> guidance to take me to this level, I couldn't possibly know what I am talking about!

Well, to those that may wonder just how these writings came about, I'd like to say this!

I received these words, phrases and sentences through my earnest desire to seek the Holy Spirit and use him as my guide. I began my training in the things that I speak about here when one day, I decided to be quiet, sit still and listen to just what God had to say to me concerning my life. My experience includes seeing my Great-grandmother get down on her knees every night to pray. She did this all the way up to the week that she died – well into her nineties. I used to listen through my bedroom door each night and hear my mother talking to the Lord, saying "Lord, please let me live to see my daughters get graduated from school and get married". And last, but not inclusive of all the experience that I've gained, I went to a little bitsy church on Pryor Street called Blessed Martin in Atlanta and played the scrub board with a spoon, while others were beating the tambourines and dancing and speaking in tongues! You see, even as a young child, I began to feel things happening all around me!

Yes, my friends! I've had plenty of experience; but, it wasn't until now that I decided to 'BREAK OUT' of my shell and put to good use, this experience that I've gained. It wasn't until now that I decided to put my Faith Degree in action. It took me a mighty long time to reach back into my past and put the heart breaks and mistakes that I've made in my life to good use; but, the Holy Spirit said "NOW, IS THE TIME!"

When I write, I don't proclaim to be none other than a writer, who decided to share a Woman's message. When I'm speaking, I don't proclaim to be none other than a spirit-filled speaker. When I'm listening to one of my Sisters that is hurting, I don't proclaim to be none other than a Sister-in-Christ. I'm just a *common* Woman, who decided to get up off the couch and do some CHANGING about the situations around her.

Have you ever heard the saying, "a tight fist can't let nothing in or out". Well, ladies for the longest my spirit was like a tight fist. My spirit was a tight fist, until I decided to release my grip a little bit. And, when I opened my hand to release the grip of hopelessness, confusion and lack of prosperity, I immediately began to grab for something else. I began to grab for something, anything that would make a difference in my life. And you know what? I caught it! When I finally opened up and began to grab for the things that I believed that I should have, I became blessed. Now, I have always believed that I deserve more in life and many times I've talked the talked about how I was gonna get what I deserve and how it was gonna be when my ship came it. But, this was just as I said, just a bunch of talk. However, when I became determined to get more, through and by the Word of God, I got it! *And I got it through the Word of God!*

Now, much like a lot of you, I didn't begin the way that I ended and I can't tell you that I went about getting what I wanted in those beginning stages, in the most righteous way. But, after it was all over, said and done, I came right back to where I started. I picked up my Bible and began to read stories about women in there. I took the time to learn about Lydia, Dorcas and even Jezebel! I took the time to read about Mary, Martha, Ruth and the Queen of Sheba. And, you know what? Through and by the Holy Word, I received my confirmation. I received the confirmation that there was more to me than meets the eye. I received my Power! My Power was given to me through my meditation of the Holy Scriptures and applying them to my daily life.

Oh Ladies! When we grab and take hold of the glory that is due us through and by the righteousness of God, we begin to exercise our Power. We can't get it, if we don't open up our minds and our hearts for it. Because just like a closed fist, nothing will enter our spirits until we open up and let it in.

I look at the publication of this book as being a new beginning for me and after your taking time to read it, I hope that this will spark a beginning of a new era for you as well. A new beginning can start now. It doesn't matter what we didn't know in the past – today, starting, grabbing and taking hold of our God-given ability is what we should focus on and I'm so glad that I found this revelation to share with you. This message that I relay to you in this publication is for the young, the old, the rich, the poor and the middle class – it is for ALL women. Its message expands the globe – there are women who suffer everywhere!

You know, I didn't realize when I started writing this journal back in August of 2001, that it would mean so much to so many people. Little did I know that even way back then, when my life was in shambles and I hadn't a clue as to what my true purpose in life was, that God's plan was for me to write about the Power within the Woman. Sometimes, I even wonder about the things written about here and wonder how I could not have known all along, what resided on the inside of me. I don't know how many times I professed to my family and friends that whatever is going to happen is going to happen, anyway. I can't begin to count the number of times that I had just given up on my life situations. As a young Woman who've seen and done many things, I have been given authority by the Almighty to write about these things here.

A Woman's Prayer

I praise you Lord, for you sent the message of this profound statement through me, your servant, the Woman. You showed me Power and how to tap into it whenever I needed it, and that is all the time. You created me Woman, and now I am the Woman who is able to change all circumstance around her; the Woman, who is able to withstand the storm, with patience and virtue. One who searches and finds the wisdom to extend confidence to the Male. I am the Woman... armed with Power – the gentlewoman, all because of you, heavenly Father. Amen.

Table of Contents

Chapter 1

The Beginning...

Where should I begin? How should I begin?

Genesis 1:1-5 "In the beginning, God created the heaven and the earth. And the earth was without form, and void; and darkness was upon the face of the deep. And the spirit of God moved upon the face of the waters. And God said, Let there be light; and there was light. And God saw the light, that it was good; and God divided the light from the darkness. And God called the light Day, and the darkness he called Night. And the evening and the morning were the first day."

I guess, I really should begin to explain when "*it*" all begins. Though, when "*it*" begins for me in my life may not necessarily be the time when "*it*" begins for you in life. I'm speaking of the *"good life, primetime, made in the shade"* time. Whatever you may wish to call "*it*" is totally up to you. I call "*it*" my Power Time!

Some women say the good life begins at 40. Others say life begins at 50. Some folks say you're in your prime in your 20's. But, who can be certain? And, who can be even more certain of the time when our life will reach its full potential?

If you answered, no one. You are absolutely right! No one can. No one other than YOU, that is. Only you and I can, or will ever know when we're ready; when we're ripe; when we're in season.

Therefore, only you and I can bear judgement of our selves. Only we can come to the conclusion that we've wasted our *good* years; that we have let the best opportunities pass us by or that we have just been down right trifling.

I've asked myself, why is it that there are so many women still searching for true love, endless opportunity, success and happiness in life, even when it's apparent that their time is long gone? Haven't they got a clue? "Why are they still tripping? Apparently they don't know that what they're trying to do just ain't gonna work!" "She's too old. She's gotten too fat," I think. I just don't have the energy anymore, was my excuse.

But then one day, I realized that *all* of these statements are just that - excuses! As I examine the Word, I realize one thing and one thing only - God is not through with us, yet!

> *Ephesians 1:17 "That the God of our Lord Jesus Christ, the Father of glory, may give unto you the spirit of wisdom and revelation in the knowledge of him,"*

No matter how old or young you are; no matter how experienced in life you may think you are, I'm here to tell you that if you have not yet satisfied the calling in your life - if you don't have that feeling of accomplishment - God is not through with you yet! If there is still yet another mountain to climb, a battle not yet won, a victory to triumph, you are still obligated to persevere. God has given us several ways to begin to obtain what is needed in our lives. He has fully equipped us for this perseverance. And, one of these ways is through and by God's spirit of *wisdom.*

> **As in Ephesians, the Apostle Paul says to open our minds to a world of knowledge in order to better serve him. He wants us to inhale the spirit of wisdom - the kind of wisdom that can only be taught by him.**

You know, there are a lot of us women still trying to make some things happen in our lives; there are some women, who are just beginning. And up until now, our lives can be classified as being without form, filled with darkness and void. Yes, up until now, just as in the beginning of time, we need light!

Let's take this example.

Upon walking into the house after being outside in the sunlight, there is an amount of time, in which your eyes have to adjust to the dimness or the lighting inside. It is almost as if, someone turned off the lights on you as soon as you stepped inside. The same thing happens when you get up in the middle of the night and turn a light on in a completely dark room. Your eyes have to suddenly adjust. Now, although it may feel a little uncomfortable at first when you come into these situations. After awhile, the adjustment occurs and everything is all right for you, visually. Have you ever stopped to think about what it would it be like, if the adjustment never came? Wouldn't it be an uncomfortable existence not being able to adjust? Of course it would be! For without this adjustment, we would experience a form of blindness. And, this wouldn't be a good feeling at all. Especially after being able to see, perfectly. It would be awful not to have LIGHT!

Just picture going through life, being outside or in a dark room. Just picture being a certain way all the time. Then, all of a sudden, you go indoors or someone turns on the light! Now picture what it is like to finally become adjusted, rooted and grounded into what God has in store for your life. Just look at your Power being manifested as that first time God called the first day into existence.

And let's take that first day being called into existence the first day that you began on this quest to seek the knowledge and wisdom needed to acquire the Power that is within you - "...let there be light."

⚜THE WORD WISDOM AND THE WORD KNOWLEDGE HAVE PRETTY MUCH THE SAME MEANINGS — UNDERSTANDING, INSIGHT, DISCRETION, LEARNING, ENLIGHTENMENT, ETC. HOWEVER, THERE IS ONE MEANING THAT I PARTICULARLY DWELLED ON AS I READ IT — COMMON SENSE.⚜ I thought, "why would the Thesaurus define wisdom as having common sense?" Then I begin to recollect some of my past years. I looked back at the time when I was up to my ears in debt. I had an older car. It was around 1987, and I thought to myself, "I need a newer model car". I thought of every scenario that I could to justify my going into more debt and buying another car. I thought that maybe I would be on my way to work, with the children and the car would break down (I hadn't had a day of engine trouble with it). I also thought that that I might have a flat tire out somewhere at night all alone (I had bought brand new tires). I even thought that I had read somewhere that having a newer car meant lower insurance premiums. Needless, to say, I thought of it all. Well, my reasoning finally aided me into making up my mind. I proudly held back my mortgage payment, didn't pay my light, gas or water bills and went into the dealership to purchase this new car. And you know what? I got it!

I became the happiest *fool* in the world that day!

Just as I started my "new auto" parade to my relatives and friends to show off my newest accomplishment, all of a sudden I got a vision. Now, what do you think would have crossed my mind at this wonderful moment, this magnificent occasion? The answer: Common sense! You see, even though I had thought this thing out over and over in my mind, I still hadn't used my common sense! And, if I had used even a little bit of common sense, I would not have lived a miserable existence for the next three or more years, because of the financial strain that this one so-called accomplishment had placed on my life.

Proverbs 15:14 – "The heart of him that hath understanding seeketh knowledge: but the mouth of fools feedeth on foolishness."

It is evident that I did not seek God before making my decision. It is even more evident that during this particular time in my life I lived in darkness or, so to speak, had not received light. But, if you had known me you would have sworn that I had it going on! I had a good job, made lots of money and lived in a brand new home. Meant nothing! I still lacked the ability to exercise the Power Within me! I did not have common sense – wisdom!

Some of you may think that this little episode not being the right way to go, is only a matter of opinion. I mean, most of us do this sort of thing all the time. We rob Peter to pay Paul, so to speak. We eventually get caught up and live happily ever after. Not! You never live happily ever after without obtaining the Power of wisdom within you. For without the presence of wisdom in our lives, we lack knowledge only available from the true authority of the Word – our Heavenly Father. A story in II Chronicles identifies the gaining of wisdom to obtain Power, very well:

II Chronicles 1:7-12 – "In that night did God appear unto Solomon, and said unto him, Ask what I shall give thee. And Solomon said unto God, Thou hast shewed great mercy unto David my father, and hast made me to reign in his stead. Now, O LORD God, let thy promise unto David my father be established: for thou hast made me king over a people like the dust of the earth in multitude. Give me now wisdom and knowledge, that I may go out and come in before this people: for who can judge this thy people, [that is so] great? And God said to Solomon, Because this was in thine heart, and thou hast not asked riches, wealth, or honour, nor the life of thine enemies, neither yet hast asked long life; but hast asked wisdom and knowledge for thyself, that thou mayest judge my people, over whom I have made thee king: Wisdom and knowledge [is] granted unto thee; and I will give thee riches, and wealth, and honour, such as none of the kings have had that [have been] before thee, neither shall there any after thee have the like."

Ladies, just as when Solomon received his request for wisdom, so came riches and wealth; even honor. So shall it be when we, ourselves, accept the spirit of wisdom from God. For, what is the use in having riches, wealth and honor, if not having Power? For having Power assures us of riches, wealth, honor, healing, and much more - all through and by the obtaining of wisdom laid out between the pages of the Word.

Sometimes I wonder where would I be without the setbacks in my life.

You know, those things that you sit back and wonder about sometimes such as: if I hadn't gotten married so young, if I hadn't gotten pregnant; if I had married the other guy, etc. You know what I mean. You're not gonna make me think that I'm the Lone Ranger! Well, my first love, as I would like to call it, stayed in the back of my mind much through the life of my first marriage. You see I became unhappy very quickly back then, and my only solace was sweet memories of a high school sweetheart. You know, every time my ex-husband and I quarreled I thought of this young man and dreamed of how perfect my life would have been if I had only married him. Well, I don't know what you've learned in life; but my lesson on that was "honey, the grass always looks greener on the other side". One day, I saw an old mutual friend of ours and she told me about how my Prince Charming was doing during that time. It wasn't pretty!

So, I said that to say this, ladies don't be mesmerized with the past, look at the present as if it is your only hope for a bright future. And, only this will make sweet memories of a not so happy yesterday.

All right, go get it! Get it ready! Wipe the dust off its binder. Take it off the coffee table. Run get it from your nightstand! You're gonna need it. I stand corrected! We've *long-time* needed it! It's time for us to get started. Its time to begin our journey up Power Road, making a right turn at a street called **WISDOM**!

Psalm 49:3 – "My mouth shall speak of wisdom; and the meditation of my heart shall be of understanding."

Chapter 2

The Power Within The Woman

The *Power Within the Woman* is derived from within the Word of God; and through and by that derivation, so has my inspiration to write about it. For the Bible says:

II Timothy 3:16-17 - "All scripture is given by inspiration of God and is profitable for doctrine, for reproof, for correction, for instruction in righteousness; that the man of God may be perfect (complete) throughly furnished into all good works."

When reading this scripture, I am assured that all scriptures, inclusive of this one are meant to be used to obtain the Power that is within us. Knowing that no matter where I pick up and turn to in God's word, these are words that can be used for instruction, so that we may be perfect (complete) and throughly furnished into all good works. Sisters, don't we want to be furnished and equipped into a good work? Shouldn't we want all of which we come in contact with made into good works? What about our husbands getting promoted on the job? Wouldn't that be a good work? What about someone near and dear to us get off drugs. My Lord! How about one of us getting off crack! My Lord! That would most definitely be a good work, in that case. Wouldn't it? You see, I don't want to project here that the Power is only good for people around us we can use this Power for ourselves.

We can use this Power to stop making the wrong choices in life. We can use our Power to listen and hear the voice of the Holy Spirit!

I also began with this scripture for advice and it serves as confirmation, as well. It advises me that I should consult with the Word in all of my writing, as well as assures me that each and every sentence provided is sanctioned by the Almighty. I asked the Lord to guide me through all the writings within these pages so that all that is revealed here be holy prepared to guide and assist my sisters to make use of the Power within.

I didn't go to my Pastors, or any other spiritual leaders before writing, I took their teachings and applied them - I simply sat down and asked the Holy Spirit for wisdom and direction drawing from all those teachings.

After all was said and done, I went back and asked great Men and Women of God to take a look at this message; I hope that I make them proud for it is from their patience and anointing in teaching the Word that even gave me an inkling of what the Woman can do!

Psalm 51:11 Cast me not away from thy presence; and take not thy holy spirit from me.

The Woman interacts with many people and engages in many roles in her lifetime. Working outside and inside the home is quite common for most of us. In fact, a lot of us find time to be part of social clubs and even become involved in charitable causes, which exposes us to even more people on a daily basis. In any event, the Woman has the potential to interact with several individuals over the course of her lifetime.

Now, in coming into contact with so many, the Woman has the opportunity to have an effect on each one of these persons, as well. It can be in a negative way or a positive way.

Nevertheless, she has the opportunity to have an impact on a life. Whether or not she chooses to use this opportunity is strictly her choice. It remains however, that the opportunity lies there - the opportunity to communicate some of her self into some one else.

2 Thessalonians 2:15 - "Therefore, brethren, stand fast, and hold the traditions which ye have been taught, whether by word, or our epistle"

This Power to impart into the life of another moves through communication. The scripture above, written by Paul was to remind the people of the things that he'd told them in the past. This communication was much needed due to what was expected of them at the coming of Christ. Below is another scripture by Paul where he used his ability to communicate to get his point across concerning the kingdom of God.

Acts 19:8 – "And he went into the synagogue, and spake boldly for the space of three months, disputing and persuading the things concerning the kingdom of God."

Now, in our case, I'm sure that there are a lot of you out there that at one time or another utilized the communication part of the Power with you. Whether you've coerced your husband just a tad or whether you simply called your creditors and made arrangements to pay your light bill, you've utilized communication to exercise your Power! And, I can't say that all of my communication has been for the good of man like Paul's, either.

But, I can say that since way back, I've realized that there is something in the Power of the tongue!

Let us rely on our ability to communicate to persuade and convince others for <u>goodness</u> sake. If diligently exercised, this vital key of communication will release the Power within us to operate in our lives and impart a positive outcome in all of our circumstances.

Further, our interacting with others is different from one to another. We communicate differently to our mothers, sisters, girlfriends and daughters than we do to our fathers, brothers and sons. ✄To put it simply, the Christian Woman may have a different advisement for each of the persons that she comes in contact with.✄ For example, our Power exercised through communication to our mothers, sisters, girlfriends and daughters may simply mean *not* to spread gossip, negativity or speak bitter words about others.

Psalms 141:3 – "Set a watch, O LORD, before my mouth; keep the door of my lips."

Our conversation should be pleasant with our sisters in Christ; therefore allowing for an atmosphere free of confusion and turmoil in our day-to-day lives. There's nothing so awful as picking up the telephone to hear a friend whose entire conversation is negative. She's either talking about somebody doing her wrong or something going wrong with somebody else. Whew! I don't know about you, but I wish that I could just lay the phone down and pretend that I never picked up! All this is an example of communicating in the wrong way!

When we utilize our Power through communicating with our Brothers in Christ, we should be careful as not to communicate the wrong message. I know that it is so easy to get what we want, when we want it from some of our male counterparts. But, though this is easy, it is also just as easy to commit a sin through this form of verbal transmitting. You may say "What is wrong with getting what I want from a man, who obviously wants the wrong thing from me?" The Word answers this by saying:

> *Proverbs 26:23 – "Burning lips and a wicked heart [are like] a potsherd covered with silver dross"*

The Amplified Says:

> *Proverbs 26:23 – "Burning lips [uttering insincere words of love] and a wicked heart are like an earthen vessel covered with the scum thrown off from molten silver [making it appear to be solid silver]."*

Ladies, if you tell lies, pretend and con your brother in order to get what you want, then you are like a vessel covered with the scum thrown off from molten silver. This is real ugly!

Also, remember the story of Jezebel.

I Kings 21:7-9 – "And Jezebel his wife said unto him, Dost thou now govern the kingdom of Israel? arise, [and] eat bread, and let thine heart be merry: I will give thee the vineyard of Naboth the Jezreelite. So she wrote letters in Ahab's name, and sealed [them] with his seal, and sent the letters unto the elders and to the nobles that [were] in his city, dwelling with Naboth. And she wrote in the letters, saying, Proclaim a fast, and set Naboth on high among the people: And set two men, sons of Belial, before him, to bear witness against him, saying, Thou didst blaspheme God and the king. And [then] carry him out, and stone him, that he may die."

Now, if it would not have been for that communication by Jezebel, Naboth would not have been killed. He would not have been killed due to the greed of her husband Ahab. And through and by this greed, Jezebel took it upon herself to forge letters and send them out to communicate an evil plan. These letters were sent to the elders and nobles who all dwelt with Naboth in his city. In other words, her communication caused his own people to turn against him. But, did she get away with it? In I Kings, it describes her demise:

> *I Kings 21:23 – "And of Jezebel also spake the LORD, saying, The dogs shall eat Jezebel by the wall of Jezreel."*

Jezebel certainly used her Power to diabolically scheme up a plan through the art of communication. However, because of her misuse of this particular Power, dogs would eat her body by the wall of Jezreel. Don't let this happen to you. Oh, I'm sure that dogs won't eat you; but, without the Almighty's shield, you may wish you had been eaten.

> *Psalm 17:3 "Thou hast proved mine heart; thou hast visited [me] in the night; thou hast tried me, [and] shalt find nothing; I am purposed [that] my mouth shall not transgress."*

What about our husbands?

Our God-given right to be a help meet to our Husbands is divine. Help meet is defined in Easton's Bible Dictionary as a 'help, as his counterpart, a help suitable to him, a wife.'

> *Genesis 2:18 – "And the LORD God said, It is not good that the man should be alone; I will make him an help meet for him."*

And therefore, we should acknowledge the divine position that he has bestowed upon us.

Before I began to write, my husband L. C. said to me that he had to tell me something that was gripped deep down in his spirit. Not knowing how I would react to what he had to say, he sat and diligently considered his words, while expressing himself to me. He sat and carefully thought out how to express to me, what God had revealed to him. When he began to speak, I sat in amazement. For what he told me is what I already knew! I needed to express in words, on pages, in binding, the Power held within each Woman of God! And through and by my Lord and Savior Jesus Christ, to the best of my ability, I shall!

1 Corinthians 11:3 – "But I would have you know, that the head of every man is Christ; and the head of the Woman is the man; and the head of Christ is God."

I, myself, am no well-educated scholar. I don't consider myself all that knowledgeable in all the ways of the World; nor, am I well versed in many other things and, I certainly can't quote most the scriptures of the Bible, right off the top of my head. However, a vision was given to me concerning the Power that I held inside of me, a long time ago. And, for many years I have had a burning desire to utilize this Power, but didn't know how. Oh, I prayed diligently and read my Bible (mostly Psalms); but with little or no understanding at all.

You see, for so many years, I have held my inner self-captive, without even realizing it.

I limited myself to what little understanding of the Word that was told to me by others and I simply read scriptures from Psalms that others told me to read to handle most situations in my life. I'll be the first one to say, I was pitiful!

But since then, I have began to execute the tasks that God had intended for me to accomplish in life since before I was conceived. Now, I feel that it is time that all wisdom and knowledge come forth and be useful in my life! I need it! It is much needed for all those that I love and cherish. This may seem a little strange for some of you; but I identify this task with a burning desire to always make things right. I used to wash and wash a pot, until its bottom gleamed; I scrubbed and scrubbed the tub until the enamel went dull. All this is what I've done in an effort to re-route the negative energy that sometimes filled my belly. I always felt that I had to let go; but, must I let go, would be my reply? Ladies, exercising the Power Within me **made** me let go!

Now, this Power inside of us should be perceived as something special and it is accomplished through

and by diligently and consistently proclaiming - taking hold - of the Word of God.

When this happens, you began to receive the help of the Holy Spirit. On the following pages are scriptures to assist in creating a foundation. They provide the evidence of why we know that there is such a thing as this Power written about here; and that we should most definitely utilize it. They should lead and guide us down a path, which holds no boundaries to our happiness, wealth, success, and salvation of our loved ones and healing.

They are:

MAN AND WOMAN

Genesis 2:23–24 "And Adam said, This is now bone of my bones, and flesh of my flesh: she shall be called Woman, because she was taken out of man. Therefore shall a man leave his father and his mother, and shall cleave unto his wife: and they shall be one flesh."

1 Peter 3:7 – "Likewise, ye husbands, dwell with them according to knowledge, giving honour unto the wife, as unto the weaker vessel, and as being heirs together of the grace of life; that your prayers be not hindered."

POWER

Ephesians 3:20 – "Now unto him that is able to do exceeding abundantly above all that we ask or think, according to the Power that worketh in us,"

2 Samuel 22:33 – "God is my strength and Power: and he maketh my way perfect."

Ecclesiastes 5:19 – "Every man also to whom God hath given riches and wealth, and hath given him Power to eat thereof, and to take his portion, and to rejoice in his labour; this is the gift of God."

Roman 15:13 – "Now the God of hope fill you with all joy and peace in believing, that ye may abound in hope, through the Power of the Holy Ghost."

Matthew 9:6 – "But that ye may know that the Son of man hath Power on earth to forgive sins, (then saith he to the sick of the palsy,) Arise, take up thy bed, and go unto thine house."

WISDOM AND UNDERSTANDING

Exodus 31:3 – "And I have filled him with the spirit of God, in wisdom, and in understanding, and in knowledge, and in all manner of workmanship,"

Psalms 119:125 – "I am thy servant; give me understanding, that I may know thy testimonies."

Job 28:28 – "And unto man he said, Behold, the fear of the Lord, that is wisdom; and to depart from evil is understanding."

Proverbs 3:13 – "Happy is the man that findeth wisdom, and the man that getteth understanding."

Proverbs 4:7 – "Wisdom is the principal thing; therefore get wisdom: and with all thy getting get understanding."

Proverbs 10:13 – "In the lips of him that hath understanding wisdom is found: but a rod is for the back of him that is void of understanding."

Colossians 1:9 – "For this cause we also, since the day we heard it, do not cease to pray for you, and to desire that ye might be filled with the knowledge of his will in all wisdom and spiritual understanding;"

2 Timothy 2:7 – "Consider what I say; and the Lord give thee understanding in all things."

STRENGTH

1 Chronicles 29:12 – "Both riches and honour come of thee, and thou reignest over all; and in thine hand is Power and might; and in thine hand it is to make great, and to give strength unto all."

Psalms 68:35 – "O God, thou art terrible out of thy holy places: the God of Israel is he that giveth strength and Power unto his people. Blessed be God."

ALL THINGS ARE POSSIBLE

Genesis 18:14 – "Is any thing too hard for the LORD? At the time appointed I will return unto thee, according to the time of life, and Sarah shall have a son."

Luke 18:27 – "And he said, The things which are impossible with men are possible with God."

Jeremiah 32:27 – "Behold, I am the LORD, the God of all flesh: is there any thing too hard for me?"

Matthew 19:26 – "But Jesus beheld them, and said unto them, With men this is impossible; but with God all things are possible."

* * *

child. After having two so close together, "It's time to put the playing to the side and learn how to do this thing right!" I thought. And my third son, who arrived many years later turned out to be my "reality check" child. For, this is the son, whose teen years, mark my searching and grabbing at the "Power" within me.

Now, just like a lot of you, while my kids were growing up I had my mother to consult with when I needed advice on taking care of them. And this was a very good thing. But, suppose just as right now in some of your lives, there isn't any one around to consult with on a daily basis; no one that you can ask even the simplest questions pertaining to raising and training your child. This is where your Power comes in. My Sisters, I just want you to know that there is hope for those of you who feel all alone.

> *Roman 15:13 – "Now the God of hope fill you with all joy and peace in believing, that ye may abound in hope, through the Power of the Holy Ghost."*

And the Amplified says:

> *Roman 15:13 – "May the God of your hope so fill you with all joy and peace in believing through the experience of your faith that by the Power of*

the Holy Spirit you may abound and be overflowing (bubbling over) with hope."

May the God of your hope fill you.

I realize these three sons of mine are blessings from God. And even though I sat depressed, many a night, because I could no longer go out to the clubs and party, hearty, there always resided a tiny spark of hope inside of me. Hope of a new day, when they would grow up and become self-sufficient. Even while I watched them run through the house hitting and screaming at each other, I always kept that splinter of hope. Now while I kept hope to be able to do the worldly things like get out the house and have a good time, it is also needful to gain hope through and by the scripture to fulfill the calling that God has for your life.

I consider myself well experienced in partying, drinking and smoking; therefore, it would benefit you well to listen to what I have to say. My lack of hope for the righteous ways of life had put me deep into a pit. I longed so much to put on my mini skirt and go to the Club on Saturday night. It broke my heart, not to be able to sit at the bar at my favorite night spot. This just goes to show you that the hope that we sometimes have is the hope that does not and never will serve us in a good fashion.

Hope is defined as: expectancy and the word Faith is defined as: assurance and trust. So in other words, this scripture is saying to us:

**May the God of our *expectancy* fill us with joy
and peace in believing through the experience
of our *trust* that by the Power of the Holy Spirit,
we may be bubbling over with our expectancy.**

The expectancy for you may be that your sons or daughters
quit smoking marijuana – mine was that my sons would stop
making the wrong choices and become productive citizens.
It may be that your husband gets saved. We don't always
live in expectancy relating to our children, but sometimes to
our counterpart.

Hallelujah! Whatever, the expectancy be in the life of
the kids, husband or any other family member be, can be
done through you putting in service Roman 15:13.

Any oppression that surfaces in your life today can
be removed by the Power Within you. And, the Power
Within you jumpstarts with the hope of a brighter future!

Chapter 4

Are We Truly Blessed?

One day, I looked at my checking account balance and said to myself, "Boy, am I blessed!" I guess this may seem a little strange to you, since you are reading my book entitled "Power Within The Woman", huh? I guess you're saying, "Well, shouldn't she be?" But, I'm not talking about being blessed through and by the Power, here. As, I stated, I looked at my *checkbook* and made this presumption. Now, I'm not trying to play on you with words, here; but I *am* trying to get you to ask yourself, in your situation, the same question. Look in the mirror at your fine figure and long beautiful hair; look at your shiny new SUV; even take a look at the beautiful home that you just purchased and ask yourself, "Am I truly blessed?"

YOU WOULD PROBABLY SAY "YES!" RIGHT? IF I WERE A BETTING WOMAN, LIKE I USED TO BE, I'D BET YOU WOULD. BUT, THIS IS ALL RIGHT, I FEEL YA! I JUST WANT TO HIP YOU TO A REAL BLESSING! YOU KNOW IT HAPPENS TO ALL OF US AT ONE TIME OR ANOTHER; WE TELL OURSELVES AND OTHERS THAT WE ARE TRULY BLESSED! I EVEN KNOW OF MY SISTERS ON THE STREET, RIGHT NOW, THINKING IN THEIR HEARTS THAT MAKING $500 TO $800, A NIGHT IS A BLESSING. MY BROTHERS, MAKING $1,000.00 TO $1,500.00 A NIGHT SELLING

CRACK MIGHT THINK THAT THEY ARE TRULY BLESSED, TOO. YES, WE ALL HAVE TOLD OURSELVES AT ONE TIME OR ANOTHER THAT WE ARE TRULY BLESSED.🕊

I'm going to take you way back for minute. Don't worry, I'll bring you back!

When I was a little girl growing up in a single parent home, I didn't feel that I missed out on the influence of a male role model. Despite, not having a father figure in the home, I still felt that I was blessed. You see, my Father happened to remain a permanent fixture in my life, even though he and my mother did not remain a couple. And, me not realizing that this was not the way that relationships were supposed to be, I grew up well adjusted in my female-run environment. (I lived with my mother, older sister and great-grandmother.) I saw my father often, talked with him by phone each night before bed and spent each summer with him. I had wonderful brothers and a beautiful step-mom, as I remained shielded from the ways of the outside world. I felt that my life was complete and the way that it was supposed to be. I would have considered myself truly blessed back then.

When I grew up. I began to meet guys, who promised me the world; but gave me nothing. I married my Prince Charming. After which, he turned into a frog. I looked for several others; but all I found were several needles in the haystacks. I began to wonder about life. I had a good job, food to eat and decent clothes. So, it was no question despite all that I went through that I was truly blessed, right?

When adulthood came, I tried matrimony, I was divorced in a year. Then and only then did I began to wonder, was I truly blessed? Yes, it took all those ups and downs throughout my life for me to finally get down to the real nitty gritty. The Bible tells us that:

Proverbs 10:22 The blessing of the LORD, it maketh rich, and he addeth no sorrow with it.

Pointing out these particular episodes in my life assists me in setting the stage, even more, for you to see the purpose of the Power. And even if your stories don't quite match mine, I believe that we'll have enough in common for you to relate to each of the situations, I express here.

I feel that there is enough of a coincidence to show that the true form of blessedness can be disillusioned, covered up and camouflaged in order that we mistake our existence for a complete and Power-filled existence.

Because even though we have fun and live, what we consider, a pretty good life, the blessing of the Lord making us rich, it NEVER addeth sorrow! It took me a long time to actually comprehend this scripture and it may take you quite some time as well. But, my meditation on this scripture reveals to me that just because good things are happening does not necessarily mean that we are being blessed! Because my good checkbook didn't last; I believe about a week later, my account was overdrawn. My good job, with a good salary didn't last. And I could go on and on and on. Even, when I went out with men that showed me a mighty good time, who paid my light bills every once and a while and even some that bought me stuff. Guess what? It didn't last and it added much sorrow to my life. ❦THOSE TIMES, YOU MIGHT SAY, WERE MORE TROUBLE THAN THEY WERE WORTH!❧

When I began to make my change, to become empowered; this is when I realized that over the years I had not been blessed, but simply led through the façade of a rose-colored world. I was led by my own will and not by God's. I followed my own wants – wants of the carnal world.

> *Romans 8:4 That the righteousness of the law might be fulfilled in us, who walk not after the flesh, but after the Spirit.*

And even though things were never really all that great in my life; my thinking was so limited that I thought that they were. For many years, I was shielded because I didn't know any better. This scripture had me covered:

> *Luke 2:8 And there were in the same country shepherds abiding in the field, keeping watch over their flock by night.*

I feel that I was like one of those sheep, being watched over by the Shepherds. You see the Lord is my Shepherd and there were several out there waiting to destroy me; but he wouldn't let them have me. There was drugs, unsanctioned sex and all kinds of immoral situations. But, I was watched over. I was watched over until I was led to gain the Power! Yes, until the Holy Spirit led me to my Bible, I was simply being watched over. And I thank God that I was!

I WANT EVERYONE READING THIS BOOK TO KNOW THAT ABUN-DANCE MAY COME IN OUR LIVES; WE MIGHT EVEN LIVE PRETTY GOOD FOR A WHILE. BUT, IF WE DON'T SEEK THE WORD OF GOD, IT CAN ALL VANISH AT THE DROP OF A HAT. I WANT TO EXPLAIN THAT THE POWER THAT IS WITHIN ASSURES US THAT THIS ABUNDANCE WILL LAST; IT CAN ENSURE THAT YOU NEVER FALL BEHIND ON THAT CAR PAYMENT. IT CAN ENSURE THAT YOUR OUTWARD BEAUTY CONTINUES AS YOU GROW OLD GRACEFULLY. IT CAN ENSURE THAT YOU MAKE THE RIGHT DECISION IN CHOOSING A MATE.

Ask yourself this infinitive phrase, this short question - Am I truly Blessed? And, just wait a second or two and rec-ollect on the good, the bad and the way life should always be. Isn't it time for you to get the Power – the Power that guarantees blessedness?

Psa 1:1-3 Blessed [is] the man that walketh not in the counsel of the ungodly, nor standeth in the

way of sinners, nor sitteth in the seat of the scorn-
ful. But his delight [is] in the law of the LORD;
and in his law doth he meditate day and night.
And he shall be like a tree planted by the rivers of
water, that bringeth forth his fruit in his season;
his leaf also shall not wither; and whatsoever he
doeth shall prosper.

Chapter 5

God's Plan

vs.

My Plans

— or —

**The "I'm gonna do what I wanna do"
Chapter of My Life!**

You know what? God knew that at some point, *"I was gonna do just what I wanted to do in life!"* He knew that I would be stubborn and disobedient and run around and not be able to do much of nothing! And, he also knew that all the things that I went through I was going to go through. And, he knew that I was going to continue to go on about my way. Until now, that is! You see, this revelation of the Power that was held within me was all part of His plan, too. His plan, which was predestined for exposure to the World in the year 2004!

> *Ephesians 1:5-6 (KJV) – "Having predestined us into the adoption of children by Jesus Christ to himself, according to the good pleasure of his will, to the praise of the glory of his, wherein he hath made us accepted in the beloved."*

Now, look at me! Here I am, at a wonderful age; but, just now able to reach inside of me and employ this God-given destiny. I'm just now able to collect that bounty held on my life; reap my reward; and just downright release all that good stuff that was stuck way down deep inside of me. Just at the right time, too. Or is it long overdue? Just why did it take so long for me to obtain this wonderful wealth of miraculous Power? After all, I needed this Power fifteen years ago, ten years ago, even five years ago when I thought my life was in critical condition. So, why is it that I hadn't already obtained what I've so diligently written about here? Well, I could give you my answer – the world's answer; but the more suitable answer lies between the pages of the Word.

In Ephesians, Paul wrote that God predestined (planned for us) to be adopted (revealed) as children by Jesus Christ to himself. In other words, God mapped out our future before Jesus ever came on the scene then had it revealed to us through and by the life of Jesus. You see God's will for us was to receive his favor, glory and goodness. He wanted us to enjoy life to its fullest. Therefore, he sent Jesus as a living sacrifice for our redemption. Hallelujah!

Now, even though God pre-planned our life for us, he knew that some of us would go and do our own thing. He knew that some of us would go out in the streets, looking for love in all the wrong places. Sister, He knew that you'd go through that nasty divorce – having your children taken away from you; go through having to bury a loved one; be

there to watch the terminal illness of another; and even witness a healing of yet another. He knew all this. But, although
God planned our future, He didn't plan those sorrowful
events to occur in our lives. All those unfortunate incidents
that took place at different times in our lives DID NOT
come from the Father! We took care of that part of life, ourselves. How? It clearly states in the Word, that God gave us
freewill (freedom of decision). Read:

> *Ezra 7:18 (Amplified) – "And whatever shall
> seem good to you and to your brethren to do with
> the rest of the silver and the gold, that do after the
> will of your God."*

And,

> *Genesis 24:54-58 (Amplified) – "Then they ate
> and drank, he and the men who were with him,
> and stayed there all night. And in the morning
> they arose, and he said, Send me away to my
> master. But (Rebekah's) brother and mother
> said, Let her stay with us a few days – at least ten;
> then she may go. But (the servant) said to them,
> Do not hinder and delay me, seeing that the Lord
> has caused me to go prosperously on my way.
> Send me away, that I may go to my master. And
> they said, We will call the girl and ask her (what
> is) her desire. So they called Rebekah and said to*

her, Will you go with this man? And she said, I will go."

In both these instances in the Bible, choices were given. Just as we are given choices in our lifetime, so was Rebekah and Ezra. Freewill is available to us do whatever we may decide to do. You see, when God laid out our destiny, we still had the opportunity to cause a few mishaps along the way. In a lot of instances, our right to make our own decisions may have caused havoc in our lives. I know it did in mine! I don't know how many times, I have gone and done the wrong thing. Knowing good and well that this is not what I should be doing. ❧ BUT, AT THAT TIME, MY PLANS WERE THE ONES GOVERNING MY LIFE. ❧ And, no matter how jacked up my plans were, you, my mother nor my Aunt Annie Ruth could have told me that these plans were not in the best interest of my life, future or success. I was living destructively! Oh, I wasn't on drugs or at least I would not have admitted to it. Because in my mind, smoking a little marijuana here and there wasn't an addiction. In my mind, having to have a glass of wine after dinner and a drink at night before going to bed, wasn't a dependency.

Let me tell you, I was so far from what God had pre-destined for me that it was a joke. I don't mean little decisions, either. I made some huge future-altering decisions back then. All which could have lead to a pitiful demise.

But, thank God that I found out and took hold of this pre-planned life given to me by God. One in which we could still be redeemed through and by the life of Jesus.

You see, when Jesus *did* arrive, all favor and mercy, according to His will, arrived as well. And, just as it was revealed that we would be forgiven for our sins and trespasses, through Jesus, this Word also reveals to you that God gave us Power to be blessed through his grace. How? The Word goes on to say:

Ephesians 1:7 – "In whom we have redemption through his blood, the forgiveness of sins, according to the riches of his grace;"

Thank God, for his grace, huh? Because, without it, I for one don't know where I'd be today. This scripture also says:

Ephesians 1:8 - "wherein he hath abounded toward us in all wisdom and prudence"

What is wisdom and prudence? The dictionary defines wisdom and prudence very similarly: Wisdom = intelligence, knowledge, enlightenment, *prudence*; Prudence = discretion, common sense, foresight, *wisdom*.

God meant for us to have wisdom. Don't sit around brain-dead! The wisdom and prudence spoke about in Ephesians is not something that

*we have to go to college to obtain. This was given
to us way back with Jesus. It is not something that
we have to be taught. Each and every Woman
reading this book has the knowledge and wisdom
to overtake the Devil.*

In this book, I go from the good times to the bad times
and then back to what we thought was the good times. As I
explain different scenarios in my life, do you see a pattern -
a pattern that simply describes a lack of WISDOM? That's
right! If only I had acquired the wisdom and understanding
to acknowledge the good from the bad, I would have saved
myself a lot of heartache. Having wisdom is a big part of
having Power! Power includes wisdom!

And listen ladies, if you can persuade yourself to think
that you will never over-come, that you will never meet the
right someone and even that your body will never be healed;
then by God, you can persuade a wayward son! You can persuade each and everyone around you, through and by the
Holy Ghost. An unfaithful husband and the release of his
addiction, all in the name of the Father, the Son and the Holy
Spirit!

*Acts 10:38 – "How God anointed Jesus of
Nazareth with the Holy Ghost and with Power:
who went about doing good, and healing all
that were oppressed of the devil; for God was
with him."*

As I said before, I'm not talking about going out getting your Ph.D., though that's all right, too! I'm not talking about getting on the internet and taking an on-line course. I'm just talking about tapping into the knowledge already locked up inside you.

We were given a choice in all matters. God gave us freewill. In the scripture, Genesis 24:54-58, Rebekah was given a choice. And, in giving her a choice she was able to make her own decision as to whether she wanted to go with Abraham's Servant (Eliezer) in order to wed Isaac, the son of Abraham. When we realize that we have a choice, life is so much better. Read more about this particular incident in the Bible, in Genesis Chapter 27.

My God! As you sit, or relax, while reading through the pages of this book, become convicted by the proof of the Word of what God's plan is for you. His plan, plain and simple, corroborates the existence of the Power within you. For without the pre-destined, redeeming, Power that he has already bestowed upon us through Jesus Christ; we would not/could not begin to handle life's trials. Furthermore, this wisdom and common-sense favor that he has bestowed on your life makes it all possible to THINK and pull out that knowledge and use it to begin to make a change. You may think that you *couldn't* handle life's trials. At least, not before now; but, let me tell you something, this Power can rise up out of you by speaking it – calling it forth.

> *Roman 4:17 "As it is written, I have made thee a father of many nations, before him whom he believed, even God, who quickeneth the dead, and calleth those things which be not as though they were."*

Read this scripture many more times; it begins one of the most, if not the most, important steps in applying your Power in everyday situations and even your most trying situations. You'll need to memorize this scripture, especially the last phrase.

There are so many things in your life that you may not see through your physical eyes. There will be many times when you may not be able to comprehend just how you're going to make ends meet or work out a problem; but, this scripture is confirmation that God will work it out for you. The Lord will bless you and I mean truly bless you.

Ladies, once we begin to accept what God has planned for our lives and stop carrying out *our* own plans during our lifetime, our Power will begin to seep through. When we begin to exercise what Paul explained to us about the Father's plan for us, we will exercise the Power available within us.

Remember, God planned for good things to take place in our lives! So, when any evil thing con-

fronts our well being (such as over-due bills, sickness, and lack), we need to use our Power to wipe out those plans. When you find yourself not being able to do without that joint every night, before you go to bed, use your Power! YOU take hold of the situation and begin to utilize the plan that God has pre-destined, girlfriend.

Right now take out your calendar, I want to you mark some dates – make some plans. For every day, from this day forward, pencil in what you're going to do: **"WHATEVER GOD HAS PLANNED FOR MY LIFE!"**

Chapter 6

The Personality Trait

Shhhh!

Can you keep a secret?

Well, if you can, I'd like to tell you a little something about myself.

Now, what I'm about to reveal to you may or may not come as a surprise; however, I take delight in exposing this little piece about me! Because I want you to have a some-what clearer picture of the Woman behind this story.

When I decided that this *Power* message had to be told -- I couldn't keep it to myself any longer -- it became my responsibility to not only tell the story, but to tell you about myself, as I go along. You see, it wouldn't be fair, to allow any mis-conceptions to begin to wander pertaining to the female behind this pen. So, it is in this chap-ter that I want to make known to all of you just who, you've so graciously allowed to speak to you from within these pages.

First off, I would like for you to know that I am just the girl next door, your average run-of-the-mill Woman;

who simply decided to confess what was deep inside her heart. The only difference that I may have from any of you is the fact that my confessions are printed and scattered throughout the world, published, for everyone to see. I was brought up in the Hood, in northwest Atlanta in Herndon Homes and am proud to let everybody know that I've never had the finer things in life. I'm proud to admit that there was a part of town that I never saw, until I turned 20 years old and I may have even been older than that; because citified girls didn't invite ghetto girls to their house, no matter if you worked with them or not! I only frequented Fourth Ward, Summer Hill and Eagan Homes, but I had a hunch that there was a Buckhead, a suburb of Atlanta, and I dreamed one night that there might have even been a more ritzy neighborhood than that. But, alas it was just a dream.

Later on though, my mother got a raise and I believe that it was that time she exercised her Power and moved us to East Atlanta. I don't remember it being much different; only though now we lived in a house and not the Projects. But even though we moved from the Hood to a real neighborhood, the Hood was still in me. I didn't really know my Power back then and continued the same mind-frame that I had grown accustomed to while growing up. Now to get you to fully understand me, let me take you back to even my younger childhood. I'll begin:

As a young child, I was known to all my family and friends as the lackadaisical, nonchalant, indifferent, one. I wasn't bothered about much of anything. I didn't let anything razz my berry, so to speak! If there was a disagreement between me and my little friends, I was usually the one that conceded and allowed the situation to go their way. I was often scolded for giving my toys away. This really got on my mother's last nerve. If I knew that I would be in trouble for not washing the dishes, I would program myself not worry about the fussing and cussing that my mother would do. I thought, "It will only last for a little while and it won't hurt me; I'll just tune it out!" I just didn't allow anything, and I mean nothing, to upset my groove. Now, don't get me wrong. I didn't let people run all over me. It is a difference in allowing something to take place versus being in a helpless situation. I never let anyone get over on me. At least, not until I got married the first time around. But, that's to talk about later.

I was a complacent child. I believe that if you would have awakened me in the middle of the night and told me that the house was in blazes, I would have simply gotten up, emotionless, put my clothes on and calmly walked outside. I didn't realize back then; but, I possessed a feeling of calm all the time. I would mindfully caution myself before any anger attack and this pretty much carried me through most of my little difficult situations. I thought this was good.

Now, this was all right and didn't really cause any major problems when I was a small child. But, I want you to imagine carrying this personality trait on up into adulthood. Doesn't seem so pretty now, does it? I mean, as an adult, at times you need to become a little aroused. Not to say that you should always blow your stack when you get upset about something. But, you should show some sort of concern about your everyday goings on. Am I right? Well, this wasn't a personality trait that I had, right off the bat. Because even after I became an adult, I not only continued to show indifference; but I subconsciously downplayed any given event and oftentimes remained emotionless when a reaction was indeed warranted. And by this time, this took little or no effort to do. You see, by now, this was my nature. It was simply my state of being.

Isaiah 32:9 – "Rise up ye women that are at ease; hear my voice, ye careless daughters; give ear unto my speech."

Once, after a strenuous weekend of partying, I was once written up at work for not showing any remorse for a report going out containing errors. My supervisor actually told me that the manager who was overseeing the proposal in which I typed and failed to proofread, was angry due to me not showing a little remorse over the horrible typing job that I had did. Honey, my head still swam; my feet still burned from the dance floor, from the night before. So, my only reply? "Too bad!"

This didn't go over well, but I didn't know any better – I hadn't received my Power.

Not realizing this personality trait causing me to project negativeness to others, would cost me several friends and job promotions, I went several years believing that I was a whole person. I was not! Because, until I realized the potential for change in my life, you might say I was an obstacle in my own path. And this obstacle caused my inability to acknowledge or feel what was needed to project a more favorable impression on those that I came in contact with. How many of you know that I had a bad personality trait? **What is your personality trait?**

It says in the Word that we should lay aside every weight. This weight in *my* life was this obstacle and weird as it may seem, the **OBSTACLE** was me and my personality trait! I was weighed down by my own thoughtlessness, showing up through my actions. Let me just break it down for you: it was showing up through my **STUPIDITY!**

Hebrews 12:1 – "Wherefore seeing we also are compassed about with so great a cloud of witnesses, let us lay aside every weight, and the sin which doth so easily beset us, and let us run with patience the race that is set before us,"

As I mentioned earlier, this personality trait lasted for years. I know some of you believe that you are the way you are, and that you have always been that way and you always will be that way. But, let me tell you something. I awoke one morning and discovered that my personality trait was not a true picture of my character. I realized that the person that I showed off as me was not me! It wasn't really who I was deep down inside; it was just an old messed up personality trait! You see my character was totally different. I was a totally different person than my personality trait led people to think I was. If you had met me, you would have called me the girl with the "attitude". I can just hear you now, "Oooh, she always has an ATTITUDE!"

I was really caring, thoughtful and attentive back then – but, my personality trait hid those traits!

This is when I realized that I had to do something. I realized that in order to bring that thoughtfulness, caring and attentiveness to the forefront, I would have to reach for that Power - that Power within me. Yes, I began to realize that everything in this life relies on us delving into ourselves and pulling out the strength that we possess inside of us.

> *Jeremiah 12:11 – "They have made it desolate, and being desolate it mourneth unto me; the whole land is made desolate, because no man layeth it to heart."*

Ladies, by not using my Power Within, I made my surroundings desolate - dismal, gloomy, unproductive. My personality trait took charge and I took a step back. In Jeremiah, the Lord declared that man made an otherwise pleasant place, a desolate one. Well, so did I! And, to top it off, man didn't even care! Ladies, I didn't care either. I remember those days back when I lived my life not using my Power; but my personality trait, instead. **I remember when I used the bat of an eye, instead of a whisper of the scripture.** And you know it would seem that I would have to have thought that my personality was not going to get me anywhere; but I didn't, because I thought that it did. I went so many years projecting the personality trait of not caring, nonchalant and lackadaisical that I thought that it was a good thing. I thought that it was cute and that I was cute for being that way. No, I don't understand why I carried that old personality trait; but one thing that I do understand is who I am now.

I am just a common Woman, who needs to have an ear to relate to this state of unproductiveness; I need an ear and a heart to meet me and agree with me on the battles that life have taken us through. Is it yours, my Sisters?

It states n the Word that God is never pleased when we do not care about something, yet we all have carried around this kind of personality trait that I spoke of. That is why this

Power that is inside of each and every one of us should be used to get rid of that slothful spirit! There are so many parts of our personality trait that can be blocking this source of our "new attitude".

Let's meditate on the Word and find it!

Chapter 7

Hold Up;
Wait A Minute!

*H*old up; wait a minute! The *Power* within the Woman is an anointed weapon. And, if you plan on using this sanctified firearm, we must first get a few things straight!

⊁FIRST OF ALL, JUST AS THE LAW OF THE LAND DICTATES, YOU'VE GOT TO REGISTER THIS BLESSED REVOLVER!⊰ Now, much like back in the day, it wasn't unusual for young women where I come from to be packin'. It still isn't that unusual in some neighborhoods, right now. So to help in getting my point across about the Power, I'd like to say that this kind of packin' that we're talking about here can and will be associated with the type of packin' that some of my sisters and I can relate to being from the Hood. Can you feel me? Because you see we used to pack because you never knew just *what you might run into*; and that holds true for today. You see, at one point in my life, there was always a degree of uncertainty; and when you are dealing with a degree of uncertainty, the natural instinct of ghetto survival requires you to have a little something extra, with you at all times. Having a degree of uncertainty today requires that a weapon be used right now as well. Read:

1 Samuel 17:45 - "Then said David to the Philistine, Thou comest to me with a sword, and with a spear, and with a shield: but I come to thee in the name of the LORD of hosts, the God of the armies of Israel, whom thou hast defied."

Hold up, wait a minute; let me tell how it all makes sense!

Even though David didn't have all the physical weaponry of the Philistines, he knew that he stood just a good of chance as they did. Because he was *"registered"* by the name of the Lord. He didn't need a spear or a shield. His shield was the simple fact that he stood behind the name of the Almighty God. Sisters, when we register our weapon with the Almighty, we are proclaiming to the World that we have everything that we need for battle. We're registered with Him. Now we're legally armed and dangerous to the enemy – the Devil.

⚔SECONDLY, YOU'VE GOT TO GET A *"LICENSE"* TO OPERATE YOUR WEAPON IN A SAFE MANNER.⚔ However, listen to me now, the time may come when you'll have to use this weapon in your self-defense. In such a case, you'll need to be well pre-pared! You'll need to be established with this Power and believe that this Power will work for you. Read this:

Matthew 21:18-21 – "Now in the morning as he returned into the city, he hungered. And when he saw a fig tree in the way, he came to it, and found nothing thereon, but leaves only, and said unto it, Let no fruit grow on thee henceforward for ever. And presently the fig tree withered away. And when the disciples saw it, they marvelled, saying, How soon is the fig tree withered away! Jesus answered and said unto them, Verily I say unto you, If ye have faith, and doubt not, ye shall not only do this which is done to the fig tree, but also if ye shall say unto this mountain, Be thou removed, and be thou cast into the sea; it shall be done."

Here, Jesus spoke words with Faith and saw results. For when he saw a fig tree in his way and saw that it was useless, he called it out of existence. His disciples were so amazed when they saw it, they marveled or were amazed at how quickly it withered away. Jesus only said to them, in so many words, if you have faith and don't doubt, you too can call something into existence, such as a mountain and cast it into the sea.

Now, if that isn't just like obtaining your license, I don't know what is. I mean, Faith is your License to make this weapon work. How else can you know, without a shadow of a doubt, that this Power is gonna work, if not only through and by Faith?

Only through and by Faith can you really be confident of the miracles that will appear in

**your life - the changes in your house, the heal-
ing of your body, the salvation of that son
or daughter! I guarantee it, cause the Word
says it!**

You know writing about the Power Within the Woman comes so natural to me, since I've utilized my female weaponry since way back. During my life's tenure, I know that I've impacted the lives of several people - a lot of whom were Men - that I love. And, I will not lie and say that all of this influence was done in good character. But, then none of you *Christian ladies* out there know where I'm coming from, do you? Well, whether you want to admit it or not, you have, too. You know what I'm talking bout. Don't be so naïve (or should I say in denial) about how you have, through and by an earnest thought process, managed to change the course of several events throughout your lifetime, simply by persuading that man in your life.

Well, just take that will and drive that you had back in those days (remember, back in the second chapter, when you were living by your plans) and turn that drive into the anointed process of registering and getting a license for your anointed weapon. Only this time, your weapon is no longer your sex appeal, it's your Faith. Your Faith pulls the trigger of your Power!

Hold up!

Wait a minute!

Now begin!

Chapter 8

The
In-Between Time

*T*here is a time in our lives when we are in-between – the in-between time.

During this time in our lives, we sit around and wait. We wait for the man to propose to us. We wait for our lucky break in the music business. We wait to win the lottery. We wait on all kinds of things. We are sort of in suspended animation, like in "The Matrix©", when the lady jumps and kicks in the air. You see every motion as she slowly floats through the air! We literally float through this stage of our lives, waiting for a miracle to happen. Don't get me wrong, I believe in miracles! But, what is evidenced in the Bible is the fact that in order to receive, we must first believe.

We are reminded in Titus 2:13 and 14 that Jesus gave himself for us.

Titus 2:13-14, "Looking for that blessed hope, and the glorious appearing of the great God and our Saviour Jesus Christ; Who gave himself for us, that he might redeem us from all iniquity, and purify unto himself a peculiar people, zealous of good works.."

When the Word says that Jesus gave himself for us, I am NOT the one to go against this. And, when it reads that he might redeem us from all iniquity, I definitely don't want to go against this. I need all the purifying and the redeeming that I can get!

At any rate, when you think of someone giving them selves for you, it should sink down deep to the core. I know that when I give of myself to a project or even to my family members, I feel that I am really doing something. I don't expect anything in return; however, I do feel like I have really done a great deed. How about Jesus? There should never be a time in our lives that we do not acknowledge this gift of unselfish love from our Father; and, accepting this, we need not lag around waiting for anything.

Ask yourself, what are you waiting for?

I spent the first fifteen or so years of my adult life in this "in-between" stage. I don't know how or when it started; but now that it's over I know that it happened. I got up every morning, got dressed, prepared the kids for school, went to work, came back home and the next day the routine started all over again. I hadn't an objective or plan to speak of, for my life; I simply existed. Well, the Father doesn't want this. You see, in order that we fully acknowledge the principle of Jesus, being a person sent here for us, we must dissolve the "in-between" period in our lives. I mean get rid of it, right here and now! Because, even if you're in the midst of it, the Power within you can remove yourself from this state.

In order to do this, we must first and foremost begin to observe <u>ourselves</u>. You see, we can examine ourselves as we do other people. I know I have a knack for looking people over. Most of the time, I just watch my unsuspecting victim. Girl, by the time its all over, I will be able to tell you if she's fake or genuine; and, I mean for real! So, just sit down and observe what it is that <u>you</u> are doing or <u>not</u> doing in <u>your</u> life. Then, get up off your rump and do something about it. It is not only healthy to do a self-evaluation; but it is also biblical. Test yourself by the scripture:

James 1:22. "But be ye doers of the word, and not hearers only, deceiving your own selves."

Are you really doing the Word?

Take another example:

Deuteronomy 4:9. "Only take heed to thyself, and keep thy soul diligently, lest thou forget the things

> *which thine eyes have seen, and lest they depart*
> *from thy heart all the days of thy life: but teach*
> *them thy sons, and thy sons' sons;"*

I realized that while I was in-between, I was so busy reading the Word – which was a <u>good thing</u> - but, I wasn't *"doing"* the Word. I wasn't doing what I was reading. So as the Word puts it:

> *James 2:20. "But wilt thou know, O vain man,*
> *that faith without works is dead?"*

I guess you might as well say that being in-between is being dead. You know what the old folks used to say, "you need not straddle the fence." Yes, you're not only straddling the fence you are perpetually frozen there. Just a short while ago, you can imagine me as being the little girl jumping rope. You know that little jump that you do when you straddle the rope and bounce from side to side.

When I began to pray and heave out all the Power inside of me to those who depend on me, I know that this Power will redeem. I know that it will redeem all that is lost in them. I know that it will recover all good things, for his name's sake. For in the word, it says that "we might be redeemed from all iniquity and purify unto himself a peculiar people zealous of good works." Ladies, we need to come out of the in-between to do this!

How are you going to call on the Holy Spirit for guidance of the Power to redeem, if you're stuck in the "Matrix"© mode?

You can't! I am so glad that through and by reading the Word, I am able to express to you what I needed for so very long. For without it, I would not even know how to begin. I couldn't begin. You know why? Because, I would be still stuck *"in-between."*

Now, let us get out of that in-between stage and get to the other side of the mountain. Trust me, it is much more pleasant there and in this case, the grass is definitely greener on the other side!

Chapter 9

Scoring a Homerun

*B*efore the women's liberation movement, a Woman's dedication was to housework, her husband and children. At home plate, so to speak, we toiled faithfully and proudly from sun up till sun down; our only ambition being to take care of our families. We did plowing and planting if we were not fortunate enough to bare many children in order to help our husbands in the fields. A large family, however, did not necessarily shield a family against poverty. For we've read in our grandparents' journals and heard stories about how they were still dirt poor.

My great-grandmother used to tell me about how common it was for you not to even have a pair of shoes until you were about 6, 7 or maybe even 8 years old. The memories of those times did not paint a pretty picture, and I oftentimes wonder if this is the reason why women were so cold and hardened in those days. I'm sure you all have heard about the mean old aunt or grandmother in the family - the one who always beat the children merciless and always spoke harshly to all the family members. I know I have. I hear tell of my great grandaunt who was part Cherokee. I used to hear my mother and aunts speak about her all the time. According to them, not only was she mean, but she was a big Woman in stature and everybody in the family was afraid of her. I wonder just what all she had to go through?! It seems that back then, when times were rough the Woman had it the roughest. These women suffered much pain and suffering, much like that which is spoken of in the Word:

> *Psalm 43:6. "Fear took hold upon them there, [and] pain, as of a Woman in travail."*

and

> *Jeremiah 4:31. "For I have heard a voice as of a Woman in travail, [and] the anguish as of her that bringeth forth her first child, the voice of the daughter of Zion, [that] bewaileth herself, [that] spreadeth her hands, [saying], Woe [is] me now! for my soul is wearied because of murderers."*

And, also:

> *Jeremiah 6:24. "We have heard the fame thereof: our hands wax feeble: anguish hath taken hold of us, [and] pain, as of a Woman in travail."*

In these scriptures, which speak of "a Woman in travail", a pain is acknowledged that is the worst pain that could befall a human being. We can pretty much summarize that this is the epitome of suffering.

Let's make comparison to a Woman's life back then and now; and, let's compare them using the concept of the all-American pastime - baseball. I know this may seem a little strange, but please, don't put the book down now; continue to read my chapter long enough to get what I'm saying.

Do you remember the Woman with the issue of blood? She went to every doctor and healer but to no avail.

Luke 8:43 "And a Woman having an issue of blood twelve years, Which had spent all her living upon physicians, neither could be healed of any,"

In other words, everywhere she went she struck out! She kept swinging, but never hit the ball. I don't know about you; but honey, I've dealt with some issues in my life! My friends could always describe me as the one "with the issues!" I used to try to belong to different organizations, I would volunteer for the March of Dimes, the Red Cross, etc. And, when God called me to join the music ministry, I took back up my clarinet and took refresher lessons and was on my way to play in the mini ensemble at Church.

But then havoc struck! During each one of these times of me attempting to share myself, give of myself, I would have a stroke *of bad luck.*

How many of you know that there is no such thing as luck? You're either in the will of God or you're not!

Well, it appeared that each time I tried to do something good in life, bad things would come out of it. My car broke down. I had such a hard time getting back and forth to rehearsal; but mostly my body became under attack. I acquired a condition that caused me to break out in hives every day! What do you think about that? There is no cure and once the allergist can't pin point any known allergen, they just call it chronic hives. Well, here I am trying to do what I think that God has called me to do and all of a sudden, I get all these issues!

Whenever I tried to break through, for example, I bought another car. Guess what? It started to give me trouble after about 6 months. And, if my car wasn't giving me trouble, my face, arms and legs would be so covered in hives and I would become so swollen that I'd be ashamed to walk out of the house! I had issues! But read this!

Luke 8:44 Came behind [him], and touched the border of his garment: and immediately her issue of blood stanched.

It was not until I touched the hem of his garment, so to speak, that I was healed from the issues in my life. Now, when the doctor says I have a condition, I say "No, I've been healed!" When the bills come in the mail with a cut-off notice, I say "They're gonna be paid!" When I get a call from friend bearing gossip, lies and confusion, I say "Sorry, you got the wrong number!"

My great-grandmother had to get up when the sun rose and sometimes even before then. She stepped up to the plate every day. Why couldn't I? Her father awakened her, since she had no brothers at home to go work with him in the field. For as long as I can remember, she told me of very cold mornings and extremely hard work – hard work that I think, being a 2000's Woman, should have never been done by a Woman. I'm all for equality and everything, but there is a difference in hard paperwork and hard physical work to me! Anyhow, my great-grandmother, did not necessarily have a physical illness such as the Woman in biblical days. And I don't think that she ever had the kind of issues that you and I are faced with, today. However, back in her day, her having to get up and go work hard in the field, in her mind was an issue! But, no matter what, each morning she arose and made it to first base – the fields.

Let me give you an example of how we sometimes handle our issues. "Today, I don't feel so well". It may simply be a mild case of cramps or a slight sore throat. I think I'll call in. It doesn't really matter about the severity of the condition or the lack thereof, I simply can't/won't inconvenience this "borrowed body suit" that I wear for just this time. ✂GUESS WHAT? WE STRIKE OUT!✂

My great-grandmother told of the time that my grandmother was in labor for two days. There was no such thing as calling the doctor and him giving you something for pain. Most times, you just went through child-bearing on your own. Even if the doctor came, he more or less supervised the birth, while you did all the work. Can you imagine having a "breech" baby all on your own? She made it all the way to 2nd and maybe even 3rd plate!

Our third example is about the two women fighting over a child.

1 Kings 3:17-27. "And the one Woman said, O my lord, I and this Woman dwell in one house; and I was delivered of a child with her in the house. And it came to pass the third day after that I was delivered, that this Woman was delivered also: and we [were] together; [there was] no stranger with us in the house, save we two in the house. And this Woman's child died in the night; because she overlaid it. And she arose at midnight, and took my son from beside me, while thine handmaid slept, and laid it in her bosom, and laid her dead child in my bosom.. And when I rose in the morning to give my child suck, behold, it was dead: but when I had considered it in the morning, behold, it was not my son, which I did bear. And the other Woman said,

Nay; but the living [is] my son, and the dead [is] thy son. And this said, No; but the dead [is] thy son, and the living [is] my son. Thus they spake before the king. Then said the king, The one saith, This [is] my son that liveth, and thy son [is] the dead: and the other saith, Nay; but thy son [is] the dead, and my son [is] the living. And the king said, Bring me a sword. And they brought a sword before the king. And the king said, Divide the living child in two, and give half to the one, and half to the other. Then spake the Woman whose the living child [was] unto the king, for her bowels yearned upon her son, and she said, O my lord, give her the living child, and in no wise slay it. But the other said, Let it be neither mine nor thine, [but] divide [it]. Then the king answered and said, Give her the living child, and in no wise slay it: she [is] the mother thereof."

As the Bible tells us, the true mother spoke up and offered her baby to the deceitful one. She was willing to give up her baby because of the lies of the other Woman. Now, this Woman, I would say definitely made a homerun. For she unselfishly would give her baby away in order to save the life of that child.

How can we make it to through the bases and score a homerun? You may say, "nobody knows the trouble I've seen"; or "I don't have time do nothing in the Church", I cant spend time with my children because I have a career"; "I can't be involved in too many things because I have to go to work and pay these bills"; and "My husband doesn't make enough money, so I have to work"; or better yet, "I am a single parent". Blah, blah, blah; the excuses go on and on. Well, you've definitely struck out! Because the Bible says:

> ***Haggai 1:5-7.*** *"Now therefore thus saith the LORD of hosts; Consider your ways. Ye have sown much, and bring in little; ye eat, but ye have not enough; ye drink, but ye are not filled with drink; ye clothe you, but there is none warm; and he that earneth wages earneth wages [to put it] into a bag with holes. Thus saith the LORD of hosts; Consider your ways."*

Yes, in all that we are doing, we must consider our ways. This is the bottom line. What ways do you have that are not pleasing in the eyes of God?

✄ I used to tend to do a little gossiping now and then. I've shown a good bit of examples here in this book. Is it a recognizable trait? I would say not! You see, we get so used to talking about each other that it becomes normal. You might say "gossip simply means to chitchat". ✄

However, it also means to deflamate someone's character or talk about someone in an unkind way. I realized that whenever I was in the presence of my husband and he gave a Woman a compliment, I had to immediately downplay the compliment. For example, if he said that someone had on a nice pair of shoes, I would immediately say, "but they don't match her outfit." If he commented that a certain friend had a kind wife, I would immediately say, "she should be, after all that she's taken him through". Do you get the picture? Consider your ways!

Now, I am probably the only person that has been a gossiper and backbiter out there, right? It's okay; I can deal with that. You see, God has brought me from a "mighty long way!"

For all of you Christian sisters that have never said an unkind word, just humor me for a moment. I've got to say my peace in this comparison to America's favorite pastime to what I believe can be a Woman's favorite pastime.

Proverbs 15:19. "The way of the slothful [man is] as an hedge of thorns: but the way of the righteous [is] made plain."

In a Woman's life, there are outfielders, infielders, catchers and pitchers; but those that can make it even to first base have the potential to score a home run. Because making it even to first base is exercising your God-given Power!

Chapter 10

Spiritual Maturity

*U*tilizing the Power within us, we Women of God have to exercise *spiritual* maturity in our daily lives. We have to do this not only for the sake of ourselves, but for the sake of our loved ones and all others that we come into contact. Now, this *spiritual* maturity comes about not by accident, nor do we simply grow old and obtain it over the years; but this *spiritual* maturity comes about through and by us seeking it, NOW. But, first we have to become aware that we lack this gift and diligently seek and secure its presence into our character and demeanor.

We need *spiritual* maturity more so now than we've ever needed it before. We need it to survive in a world where there may NOT be a Godly male figure. In other words, there may not be a Man in your life that you can depend on. I oftentimes remark that I may have been married several times; but I've only had one Husband! My Sisters, you may have come into contact with SEVERAL un-Godly Men through the course of you finding yourself. We can go through this searching stage before we receive our Power! You may have even given birth to several children by these guys. But, I'm here to tell you that it's going to be all right. Because when God made Man the head, he made him the leader of the Family; but he also made him to lead under his (God's) direction. There are so many Men that have not received that calling, yet. There are many Men, who just don't get a clue. However, this shouldn't make or break you, the Woman. Because when God created you, he also equipped you with a mind. As it says in the Bible, God took a rib of Adam and created Woman; therefore, when he created us from Man, he also duplicated the wisdom that he put into Man. He also duplicated the knowledge that he wanted for Man.

You might say that he simply cloned Man into a more feminine replica – YOU!

Yes, the Woman has the things necessary to persevere, as well; God intended it that way. So, when that Man leaves you with children to feed and bills to pay, you can still make it. You will make it with the help of your *spiritual* maturity – the only kind of maturity that can help you overcome this bad situation.

The dictionary defines the word spiritual as "pertaining to, or made up of spirit, rather than the physical body or world" and maturity as "having attained a final or desired state". Our spirit or our soul, so to speak, is viewed as distinct from our physical body. So, broken down for us: spiritual maturity is the final state that God gives us which is not of this world, but a part of us which is on another level – a more heavenly level, so to speak. I believe that in this

realm of our being, we have the ability to foresee and over-
come our obstacles. I believe that there is nothing that we
cannot overcome. Have you ever tapped into your *spiritual*
maturity? Did you even know that there was such a thing? I
didn't, until a couple of years before I began these writings!

There are several passages in the bible referring to the
word "spiritual", a couple follow:

*Colossians 1:9. For this cause we also, since the
day we heard [it], do not cease to pray for you,
and to desire that ye might be filled with the
knowledge of his will in all wisdom and spiritual
understanding;*

And

*1 Corinthians 3:1 "And I, brethren, could not
speak unto you as unto spiritual, but as unto carnal, [even] as unto babes in Christ.*

In reading these two passages, I believe that the *spiri-
tual* maturity state is reached by diligence in the Word of
God. I also believe that in conjunction with tapping into the
Power within us, we need to delve into the Word, dissect it

and earnestly seek our Father's message in order to under-stand how to make use of this maturity level. Maturity is just plain being mature; we all know this. However, being in the realm or possessing *spiritual* maturity is a step above your plain old maturity state.

> **Being *spiritually* mature can mean the differ-ence in speaking and not speaking; even acting a certain way. All this and more is accomplished when you operate in *spiritual* maturity.**

I know that when you caught your boyfriend at the Club with that other Woman, you wanted to just pull all her hair out! You might have even wanted to slash his tires, when you saw him walk hand and hand with your so-called friend at the Park. But, let me tell you something that I learned: you can do more damage and gain more success on your knees! I don't know how many times I have got a neighbor up in the middle of the night to drive me to a place, where my Husband was and take the car away from him! Yes, I did that! Once my ex-husband told me that he was going to the store and that he would be right back. ❧I KNOW THIS HAS HAD TO HAVE HAPPENED TO SOMEBODY OUT THERE!❧ Well, 1:00a.m. came, 2:00a.m., came and then 3:00a.m. came. I called one of my neighbors, you know that neighbor that you have that will always be by your side when mess is up! When you need to go to the grocery store or something, she can't be found; but, tell her that you think your Man is fooling around and she's Johnny-on-the-spot! Anyway, I knew just who my Man was messing around with and I knew where she lived and worked. I jumped in the car and my neighbor friend drove me all the way across town to an apartment complex and there sat my car! I looked up at the apartment window and all the lights were out – they must've gone to bed. Well, using my spare key I drove my car right on home. The next day, around 10:00a.m, the phone rings and guess who it was? On the other end, was a panting, out of break Man declaring to me that our car had been stolen at the Pool Hall? And he was so good he had a friend there with him to corroborate his story. I hope you know that I needed some *spiritual* maturity! Because, after this event and many other crazy incidences I continued to remain in this relationship. How many of you out there know that all marriages aren't made in heaven?

In my quest for *spiritual* maturity (I didn't know what it was back then), I spent numerous days and nights seeking for the answers that might bring about a transformation in my life. But, all to no avail! I didn't find any reasons why my relationship or love affairs didn't always pan out like a well-written movie script you might watch on T.V. Isn't it something how no matter how bad the events are in a movie, most times, there's always a happy ending?

**But, over time, I discovered that my *spiritual*
maturity lay deep within the maturity that was
already within me. I possessed the key in order
to obtain the Power and utilize my *spiritual*
maturity. I found that; however, if we do not
seek God, we may not ever be able to unlock our
spirit with this key – we might never reach this
maturity level.**

At one point of my life, it was me, me, me. Everything
had to do with me; it had to be all about me; and the situation always had to surround me. When I graduated high
school, at the age of 17, no one could have told me that I
didn't know everything there was to know about life.
Looking back at that year and several years after that one,
life's a blur. And to tell you the truth, between partying, dat-
ing and working, I cannot think of one thing that was
accomplished during that time in my life. But, I thought that
I had made it in life. At that time, I would have proclaimed
that I had reached my full potential. But listen to this: everything that I bought and paid for is no longer operating;
monies that I made have long been spent; persons that I par-
tied with I no longer am in touch with. I can remember those
things that caused an impact on my life. However, I can't
remember and to this day don't know how the things that I
have gone through marked my path to *spiritual* maturity.
My only recollection is that when I began to see within me,
to know where my life was headed and what my life means

to so many people around me is when I truly tapped into my *spiritual* maturity.

The greatest tool that a Woman can have is *spiritual* maturity. I call it my handheld tool. For without it, I couldn't go about fixing minor jobs around the house (my life). My little tool helps me in a big way. Whenever I need to tighten a screw; you know the screw that you have a hard time trying to find the right screwdriver for. Well, my tool tightens that screw and from that point forward, whatever had been loose is now tightened. Praise God!

The scripture 2 Peter 3:18 gives us words that we can use as a tool:

2 Peter 3:18. But grow in grace, and [in] the knowledge of our Lord and Saviour Jesus Christ. To him [be] glory both now and for ever. Amen.

With this tool, I find that I can pry open things.

One day, my youngest son seemed to be perplexed and for the life of me I couldn't figure out why my son seemed to be so confused, so not at peace with himself. I contemplated calling a therapist and even seeking the advice of a psychologist. But, I never did either of these suggestions, thanks to my tool. With my *spiritual* maturity, I found a lonesome young man who needed guidance in the establishment of goals for a new future. I learned a lot more about him during this small period that I'd learned over his lifetime. After all these years, I began to see just "what make him tick". Then I became able to pry open that which had been closed up so tight inside of him. All, because by this time, I had read:

> *2 Corinthians 1:6: "And whether we be afflicted, [it is] for your consolation and salvation, which is effectual in the enduring of the same sufferings which we also suffer: or whether we be comforted, [it is] for your consolation and salvation."*

I was able to loose that confusion that he had concerning where he was going to go in life and why things hadn't worked out for him in the past. I was able bring out all that was shut up inside of him by exercising my *spiritual* maturity. I was even able to assist him in bringing about his own spiritual awareness. There's still a long ways to go there, but thanks to this God-given hand tool, I was able to work like a carpenter, with his tools. I utilized my Power - the Power within this Woman!

Chapter 11

Living by Circumstance

They say that sometimes it takes a devastating experience to make one realize the most important things in life. In my case, I had several different devastating experiences; but they all proved nothing to me.

I am a lot like you; I'm one who just couldn't relate the Word of God to my everyday existence. All I could do was to live by circumstance. As far as relying on God, if I couldn't see it, I wouldn't believe it!

Everything bad that happened to me, I thought, was simply a result of my current situation. The reason that I never got caught up on my bills, I thought, was because I didn't make enough money. The reason that I kept meeting the wrong guys, I thought, was because there weren't any more good men left. The reason why I married and divorced, I thought, was because of the other woman. I had a reason, which was always circumstantial, for what was going wrong in my life.

There is a story in the Bible about a Woman whose circumstances seemed very dim. Elijah was sent to her by God; however, she was a widow woman, very poor:

1Kings 17:11 And as she was going to fetch [it], he called to her, and said, Bring me, I pray thee, a morsel of bread in thine hand.

1Kings 17:12 And she said, [As] the LORD thy God liveth, I have not a cake, but an handful of meal in a barrel, and a little oil in a cruse: and, behold, I [am] gathering two sticks, that I may go in and dress it for me and my son, that we may eat it, and die.

When I read this chapter, particularly these two scriptures, I thought about myself. There were so many days when I didn't have enough food for my kids to eat. How many of you know that when you work, most times you're going to be over the limit to receive food stamps.

Well, this was the case for me, at one time. It was almost as if I was being punished for even having a job. But, it was then that I found out that our lives don't have to be ruled by worldly circumstances. We don't have to succumb to the curses and demonic forces present around us.

The Bible goes on to say:

1Kings 17:13: And Elijah said unto her, Fear not; go [and] do as thou hast said: but make me thereof a little cake first, and bring [it] unto me, and after make for thee and for thy son.

1King 17:14: For thus saith the LORD God of Israel, The barrel of meal shall not waste, neither shall the cruse of oil fail, until the day [that] the LORD sendeth rain upon the earth.

1Kings 17:15: And she went and did according to the saying of Elijah: and she, and he, and her house, did eat [many] days.

In the widow's house, they did eat for many days. Simply by being obedient to the Word of God, a Power was exercised through this Woman. By simply heeding to the word of the Man of God – Elijah – she received an abundance in her household.

At one point in my life, it seemed that every time I took a step or two up the ladder, I fell back down three or four. I blamed it all on my current situation. I blamed it all on circumstances! It wasn't until I learned how to rise above my situations that I became blessed. It wasn't until I became aware that my circumstances was just that a circumstance.

A circumstance doesn't have to be permanent! Any other words, "Circumstances Can Change!"

Now, there are some who choose to move away from areas in which a lot of immoral things are taking place, in order to change their housing circumstances. But, if after you move to the outskirts of your City into your fine new brick home and you still pick up the phone to call and talk about Shirley; then you might as well still be in the ghetto! ✄THERE IS A WOMAN, WHO MAY DECIDE TO QUIT SLEEPING AROUND SO THAT THIS WILL CHANGE HER CIRCUMSTANCES. BUT IF THAT SAME WOMAN CONTINUES TO KEEP UP MESS ON THE JOB; THEN MY SISTER, SHE MIGHT AS WELL KEEP ON SEEING MR. JONES AND JUST KEEPING IT ON THE DOWN-LOW! I HEARD A WOMAN SAY ONE DAY THAT SHE WOULDN'T DARE MINGLE OR ENTERTAIN IN THE COMPANY OF HOMOSEXUALS; BUT AT THE SAME TIME, SHE ALLOWED HER BROTHER TO SMOKE CRACK IN THE BASEMENT OF HER HOME. AFTER ALL, SHE WOULD SAY, THIS IS MY BROTHER I LOVE HIM; I JUST CAN'T PUT HIM OUT! CAN YOU GET WHERE I'M COMING FROM? EVEN THOUGH WE SOMETIMES MAKE A PHYSICAL CHANGE, SOME OF US ARE STILL LIVING IN OUR SAME OLD BAD CIRCUMSTANCES!✄

> **If there is one thing that exercising your Power within you can do it is to get you out of your circumstances. Just think about it! If you continue to go on through life not using the God-given force to call those things that be not, as though they were, you will always live according to your circumstances.**

Even if you are one of those who have never done any more or less than what you're doing right now. You know that friend that has lived in the same house and worked the same job every since you met them? They are very comfortable in their surroundings and current situation; and wouldn't ever contemplate changing anything about the way they are living. They take the good with the bad and live on, so to speak. Even if you are one of those types, there is still that Power that needs to explore another possibility. Because even if you choose not to make a physical change, if you are not living and using the Power, you are still not living up to your potential. You may be destined for a _better_ circumstance!

Deuteronomy 5:33: Ye shall walk in all the ways which the LORD your God hath commanded you, that ye may live, and [that it may be] well with you, and [that] ye may prolong [your] days in the land which ye shall possess.

Now, I don't mean to question your circumstance, if you are well satisfied; however, obtaining the knowledge to realize whether or not you are in the ideal situation takes some tapping into your Power!

Chapter 12

Power and the Woman

*M*any persons (women and men, alike) that I have allowed to review this manuscript, before publication, have expressed to me that they have never heard these expressions of character and traits prevalent already in the Woman, referred to as "Power". I'm sure that even now, there are still questions as to the exact definition of "Power" as it relates to us Women.

Well, I added this chapter right before publication in order to more clearly clarify the meaning that I received about the Power within the Woman, so that you are able to experience the joy and satisfaction of this new, yet old characteristic of man's help mate. THE BIBLE HAS SO MANY SCRIPTURES FOR YOU TO READ OVER AND OVER AGAIN; TO SINK INTO YOUR SPIRIT IN ORDER TO CHANGE YOUR SITUATION. AND WHILE CHANGING YOUR SITUATION YOU ARE UTILIZING YOUR POWER!

I believe that God gave me the task of relaying this message to the ordinary Woman, like me! He took this common Woman, after reading the many scriptures to realize this Power, and helped me step right on out of my bad situation. He gave me the understanding and knowledge to use my Power to fight the enemy. Now, you may be like I was and say that you know you have it; but you're also just like me when the Holy Spirit said to me "your life still ain't showing it!"

I say to you that there is a relation to the successful Woman and Power. And, I don't necessarily mean successful as in being in the workplace.

❧

FOR THE WOMAN CAN HAVE SUCCESS IN THE HOME, IN THE WORKPLACE AND EVEN IN AN OTHERWISE UNPLEASANT SURROUND-ING, SUCH AS INCARCERATION. Yes, even if you happen to obtain a copy of "Power Within the Woman" and you are behind bars, whether due to your own fault or the fault of others, you can still find that Power that is within you. It doesn't matter what you did yesterday, just read:

> *1 John 1:9 If we confess our sins, he is faithful and just to forgive us [our] sins,* **and to cleanse us from all unrighteousness.**

And

> *Psalm 18:2-3 The LORD [is] my rock, and my fortress, and my deliverer; my God, my strength, in whom I will trust; my buckler, and the horn of*

my salvation, [and] my high tower. I will call
upon the LORD, [who is worthy] to be praised:
so shall I be saved from mine enemies.

There is an anointing on the lives of God's people, particularly the female. It doesn't take a rocket scientist to see that
there are so many blessed functions and duties in the life of
the Woman. Even if you are someplace that you don't want
to be, use this time to meditate on the things of God. Use
this time to read scripture, after scripture. I used to read the
Psalms all the time. If you were to ask me why, I couldn't
tell you. All I can guess is that my mind just wasn't big
enough to read through the other books. But, you know after
reading the Psalms over and over, I received a passion. I
received a passion to explore the rest of the Bible. I started
in Genesis, which I hadn't heard since I was a little girl
going to Sunday school. Then I went on to Deuteronomy
and decided that I needed to know more. The folks in there
got interesting to me. I wanted to find out about who begat
who and why they begat and on and on and on! Then I
became committed to reading my Bible.

When my ex-husband starting fooling around on me, I
picked it up and read till I fell asleep each night. When my
ex-husband got on drugs, I read it at work, when I was on
my lunch break. When my kids started to get into trouble I
read it at the breakfast table. I began to READ. And through
and by this timeline of events in my life was I able to finally
get my Power!

You may not even be experiencing anything in your life right now; but, a time may come, when you are. I don't want to scare you; but you need to stay prayed up! Don't wait until you see the clouds to start preparing for the rain! Get down on your knees and begin to pray, now! Have you ever heard the expression, a day late and a dollar short? I think that it was written for me! I've always started everything needful in my life, it would appear, too late! And, I've never had the resources to do what I needed done at the right time!

There have been a lot of bad situations happen to me in my life and the majority of them happened due to Men who didn't have God in their lives. I believe that what I'm about to tell you expands the globe when it comes to trifling Men! Not to give the Power meaning ammunition for male-bashing, but there have been a lot of strife caused in the lives of women, all over the world, due to a lack of leadership and compassion from the male. I don't care if you're black, white, rich or poor at some point in your life a male has caused you some heartache. But the Power gives you strength. The meaning of Power relates to your strength in these situations – Power can relate to your strength in all areas. Because when the male is not able to carry out what God intended him to do, as his helpmate, our Power will see us through. Our Power has a meaning now that not only biblically helps Man, but also allows us strength to continue in a bad situation. How many of you know that God doesn't want any of his people to suffer. And, even though God told us to be a helpmate to man, he does not want the un-Godly man to abuse us! Therefore, another meaning of Power – strength – will see us through!

Power as it relates to the Woman is simply using the ability that God has already bestowed upon us, whether it be alongside a Man - your mate - or not. I'm also talking to you single parent homes, where there is only the Woman there.

> *Proverbs 31:30 Favour [is] deceitful, and beauty [is] vain: [but] a woman [that] feareth the LORD, she shall be praised.*

In the many instances, where is only the female to lead and act as role model to both male and female children, God has indeed instilled the Power. For the Lord says:

> *Hebrew 13:5... for he hath said, I will never leave thee, nor forsake thee.*

The

Conclusion

This concludes my writing for now on the subject of the *Power within the Woman*. However, this should not conclude the unmistakable guidance of the Holy Spirit, present in our lives each day to assist us to forge ahead applying this Power. For there is still more ammunition stored away inside us that we haven't yet used. Yes, there is yet more to be said and more to be explored in this area. The Power never ceases, as long as we hold true to the Word. I would like to consider myself, "a work in progress". We are all works in progress and we will always be for we should never stop seeking the Power that resides within us.

I would like to thank my many editors, who submitted their comments and suggestions!

When I began these writings, little did I know how far this manifestation of God's holy plan for the life of the Woman, would take me. Little did I know how many lives, I would touch by simply writing these words on these pages. I never admitted to having any "special" talent; nor did I ever boast of a unique ability to entertain, nor enlighten the masses. However, when I began to sit in front of my much-needed, upgraded computer, something began to pour out of me. And, I hope that what has poured out of me has in some way leaked, dropped on and even stained **YOU**. I hope that the hunger for something to take hold of your life, so that you can make a change, while helping all those around you, is about to be satisfied. I hope, too that, whatever there is that is deep down hibernating inside of you wakes up!

There are so many avenues you may take in order to reach the road to your Power.

Therefore, I would like to reiterate that this is just a small sampling. My sisters, this cannot, in any way, be conclusive of what you and I may find through our search. Our success simply depends on our willingness to proceed down a long and sometimes lonesome highway; not giving up and continuing to talk it through with our Holy Comforter.

To God be the Glory!
Dorothy

To Order

For copies of *Power Within The Woman*, send a check or money order in the amount of $8.95, add $3.00 for postage and handling, to the address below:

L. C. & S. Publishing
P.O. Box 71484
Newnan, Georgia 30271-1484

Notes from the Holy Spirit

Notes from the Holy Spirit

Notes from the Holy Spirit